The Best of Encyclopedia Brown

Mysteries by
Donald J. Sobol

READ 180™

SCHOLASTIC INC.
New York Toronto London Auckland Sydney
Mexico City New Delhi Hong Kong

COVER ILLUSTRATION

PATRICK FARICY

Printed in the U.S.A.

ISBN 0-439-08279-X

1 2 3 4 5 6 7 8 9 10 23 06 05 04 03 02 01 00 99

Table of Contents

The Case of the Missing Garlic Bread

Idaville looked like any other seashore town its size—on the outside. Inside, it was like no other place in America. For more than a year, no one had gotten away with breaking the law there.

Idaville's chief of police was Mr. Brown. He had a secret. Whenever he or his officers came up against a case too difficult for them, he knew what to do. He went home and talked to his only child, ten-year-old Leroy.

Over dinner, Leroy solved the case for him.

Leroy never spoke a word about the help he gave his father. He didn't want to appear different from other fifth-graders. But there was nothing he could do about his nickname, Encyclopedia.

An encyclopedia is a book or set of books filled with facts from A to Z, just like Encyclopedia's head.

He had read more books than almost anyone, and he never forgot what he read. He was like a bookmobile that runs on peanut butter and jelly sandwiches.

From fall to spring, Encyclopedia helped his father capture crooks. When school let out for the summer, he helped the children of the neighborhood, as well.

Every morning he hung his sign outside the garage.

BROWN DETECTIVE AGENCY
13 Rover Avenue
Leroy Brown, President
No Case Too Small
25¢ Per Day Plus Expenses

One morning in late June, Encyclopedia and Sally Kimball, his partner, were seated in the garage when Josh Whipplewhite entered. Josh wore a mad and hungry look.

"You missed breakfast?" asked Encyclopedia.

"No," grumbled Josh. "Lunch."

"It's only ten o'clock in the morning!" exclaimed Sally. "You must have just flown in from France!"

"Naw, I never left Idaville," Josh replied. "But part of my lunch took off."

He explained. His mother had been fixing the food for his birthday party which was to start at one o'clock. She had made a big loaf of garlic bread and a chocolate cake. She had put them on the windowsill for a minute to get them out of the way.

"The cake and the garlic bread disappeared as if they'd flown—*pffft*!" Josh said. "My party's ruined!"

"You can have a party without garlic bread," Encyclopedia pointed out.

"But not without a birthday cake," declared Sally.

"Uh-uh," corrected Josh. "It's the garlic bread I'll miss. I'd rather have it than cake anytime."

He put a quarter on the gasoline can beside Encyclopedia. "I want to hire you," he said. "Find the thief!"

"Did you see anyone around your house at the time?" asked Encyclopedia.

"Three or four big boys," said Josh. "I didn't pay much attention. But one of them was called Bugs."

"Bugs—Bugs Meany!" cried Sally. "I knew it."

Bugs was the leader of a gang of tough older boys. They called themselves the Tigers. They should have called themselves the Pretzel Makers. They always tried to make dough the crooked way. The only things they hated more than honesty were soap and water.

Encyclopedia had dealt with Bugs in the past. Almost every week he had to stop the Tigers from cheating the children of the neighborhood.

"I'm pretty sure the Tigers made off with your garlic bread and birthday cake," he said. "Come with us."

The Tigers' clubhouse was an unused toolshed behind Mr. Sweeney's auto body shop. Bugs Meany,

Duke Kelly, Spike Larsen, and Rocky Graham were inside, sitting on orange crates and chewing parsley.

Bugs chewed a little faster when he saw Encyclopedia, Sally, and Josh approaching.

"What's this?" he called. "Winter must have come early this year. The nuts are falling out of the trees."

Encyclopedia was used to Bugs's greetings. He ignored the remark.

"This is Josh Whipplewhite," he said. "Earlier this morning you four stole a birthday cake and a loaf of garlic bread from his kitchen windowsill."

"Stole?" exclaimed Bugs. He struck his forehead as if he couldn't believe anyone would accuse him of stealing. "We've been right here in the clubhouse all morning eating rabbit food. Got to get our vitamins."

"You unwashed ape," said Sally. "You're lying."

Bugs tilted his nose. "What makes you so sure, Miss Smarty?"

"Your lips are moving," snapped Sally.

Bugs grew red. "You prove I'm not honest in word and deed, and us Tigers will buy this little whipple-dipple kid another cake and a loaf of garlic bread."

"Agreed," said Encyclopedia quickly. He moved off to the side and powwowed with Sally and Josh.

"All we have to do is sniff their breath," whispered Josh. "Garlic leaves a terrible smell."

"They thought of that," Sally said. "They're

chewing parsley on purpose. Parsley will sweeten even a camel's breath."

"Well, somebody ought to take a whiff just the same," Josh said. "But not me. It's my tenth birthday, and I want to live to be eleven."

Sally looked at Encyclopedia. The boy detective looked away. He had no desire to have his nose bitten by an angry Tiger.

"Boys," Sally said disgustedly. "All right, *I'll* do it."

She marched up to Bugs. "Open your mouth if you dare, you runaway from a bathtub."

Bugs seemed to be waiting for the command. He opened his mouth willingly.

Sally put her nose close. She did the same with Duke, Spike, and Rocky. They breathed heavily into her face and grinned.

She returned to Encyclopedia and Josh, defeated.

"The parsley got rid of the evidence, darn it," she said. "Bugs's breath is better than usual."

"There goes my lunch party," groaned Josh.

"Not yet," said Encyclopedia. "I think I can prove the Tigers stole the garlic bread and birthday cake."

HOW?

(Turn to page 53 for the solution to "The Case of the Missing Garlic Bread.")

The Case of the Bubble Gum Shootout

Encyclopedia and Sally were strolling through South Park when they chanced upon Cephas Keefer.

Encyclopedia liked Cephas, though the little fourth grader had a temper like gunpowder. When it exploded, he would do battle with anyone. Usually he overmatched himself.

At the moment, Cephas lay all alone in the shade of a banyan tree. He appeared to be giving himself mouth-to-mouth resuscitation.

His cheeks were puffing and unpuffing, his lips were puckering and unpuckering, and he was making noises like a wounded hippopotamus.

"Oh, dear," Sally said anxiously. "I think he's been punched out again." She hurried to Cephas and asked, "Who did it?"

"Nobody," Cephas answered calmly. He puffed a final puff. "I'm just warming up the old lips."

"For what?" inquired Encyclopedia. "To go three rounds with an air hose?"

"Uh-uh," said Cephas. "I've got a bubble gum shootout with Malcolm Nesbit at noon." He glanced at his wristwatch and jumped to his feet. "I better hurry."

A bubble gum shootout did not happen every day in Idaville, and so the detectives went along. Cephas, who strutted with confidence, explained how the shootout had come about.

It had begun a year ago at a baseball game. Cephas and Malcolm were in the outfield. They chased a long fly ball into some bushes and found a beautiful ten-speed bicycle hidden there.

When the two boys were unable to find the owner, they took the bike to the police station. Officer Carlson told them that if no one claimed the bike in a year, it was theirs. The year had ended yesterday, and the bike was still unclaimed.

"I guess I've been bragging too much about what a great bubble-gum blower I am," confessed Cephas. "Malcolm said he could pick anyone—even a perfect stranger—and put him against me. That made me boiling mad. I dared him to try."

"If you defeat the stranger, the bike is yours?" asked Sally.

"Yup," Cephas replied. "And if I lose, the bike is Malcolm's. But I'll win. I'm made for bubble gum. I have the lungs of a lion, the tongue of a cobra, and—"

"The temper of a tiger," Sally said. "Be thankful Encyclopedia is here to keep you from being cheated. Malcolm is tricky. He likes to eat his cake and have yours, too."

At the west end of the park, Malcolm was waiting. He greeted Cephas and smiled coolly at the detectives.

"Now I'll choose your opponent from among perfect strangers," he said to Cephas.

He ambled a hundred feet to a brick path and spoke with several passers-by. Encyclopedia could not hear what was said. The passers-by laughed, shook their heads, and strolled on.

After many minutes, Malcolm brought back a blonde girl of about fifteen.

"Meet our volunteer, Teresa Byrnes," he said.

"This is far out, wild," Teresa said. "I haven't blown bubble gum in years."

She carefully set on the ground the brown paper bag she had been carrying . "My lunch," she remarked offhandedly.

Malcolm handed Cephas and Teresa three pieces of gum each. While he went over the rules, Encyclopedia and Sally edged close to the brown paper bag.

"What's inside?" Sally whispered.

Encyclopedia peered in. "A small jar of peanut butter with a screw-on top," he answered, "and a package of paper napkins."

The shootout consisted of three events. "Whoever wins two is the victor," Malcolm declared. He gave Sally a tape measure and grandly appointed her the judge.

The opening event was to blow a bubble while somersaulting. Cephas went first and blew a four-incher.

Teresa applauded and refused her turn. "No, thanks," she protested with a laugh. "I'd break my neck."

After only one bubble, Cephas was halfway to winning the bicycle!

The second event was to blow two or more bubbles at once. Cephas failed on his first attempt. So did Teresa.

On his second attempt, Cephas got out two small bubbles. Suddenly Teresa was all business. She worked the gum in her mouth deliberately, unhurriedly—and blew three bubbles.

"Wow!" she bellowed. "What luck! What luck!"

It was one victory each.

The third and deciding event was blowing for size.

Cephas had lost a little of his confidence. He did not glance at Teresa as he took a deep breath and gathered himself together.

A thin tip of pink appeared between his lips and grew steadily into a bubble. It grew and grew until it hid his face. Gently, as if it were a ball of hammered lace, he pulled the bubble free and held it for Sally to measure. Twelve inches!

"I don't know how I did it," he gasped. "I never

blew one that big before, and I had a head wind."

Teresa seemed doomed to defeat. Yet she did not look worried. She chewed her gum slowly and worked it against her front teeth. She took her time.

The bubble appeared, growing faster than Cephas's head. It seemed ready to burst at any second. Then all at once the huge pink beauty was in her hand.

Sally measured it. Twelve and a half inches!

Malcolm grinned triumphantly at Cephas. "A perfect stranger beat you," he crowed. "The bike is mine."

"It is not," said Encyclopedia. "You cheated."

HOW?

(Turn to page 54 for the solution to "The Case of the Bubble Gum Shootout.")

The Case of the Chinese Restaurant

Oliver Wilkie was fourteen and loved Chinese food. He was known by some as the Cantonese Kid. Others called him the Subgum Submarine because of the way he dove into any dish flavored with Chinese vegetables.

Whenever he had spare cash, he spent it at the Chinese restaurant near the junior high school. Usually he bought a takeout order of egg rolls or barbecued spareribs, which he ate by the duck pond behind the restaurant.

When he rang Encyclopedia Brown's doorbell, he looked as though a toothache would make him happy.

"I need your help," he said to the detective. "I could go to prison."

"Come in," said Encyclopedia. "You'd better sit down. What's the crime?"

"I'm supposed to have stolen $108," he said. "But I didn't. The money disappeared from my schoolbag while I was in the Chinese restaurant Monday. The next day the restaurant went out of business."

"Oh," Sally said sympathetically.

"Oh, oh," corrected Oliver. "First, I'm accused of stealing. Then the restaurant folds. I've been hit with a one-two punch to the head and stomach."

"Who says you stole the money?" Encyclopedia asked.

"Mitch Landon and Kate Walters," Oliver answered. "Since I beat Kate in the election for treasurer of the Service Club, she's had it in for me. She and Mitch are very close. They play mixed doubles on the tennis team."

"What do they say about the missing money?" Sally asked.

"I haven't time to tell you now," Oliver replied. "I'm already late for my piano lesson. But Monday at three o'clock there'll be a hearing in the principal's office. Can you be there?"

"Yes, and don't worry," Encyclopedia said. "Everything will turn out all right."

He spoke encouragingly, but he didn't feel encouraged at all.

Nonetheless, on Monday he and Sally joined Oliver, Kate, and Mitch in the office of Mr. Gerard, the junior high school principal.

As the detectives found seats, Mr. Gerard gazed at them questioningly. Oliver explained why they were there. Mr. Gerard nodded his permission for them to remain.

"This is not a trial," Mr. Gerard began. He was a

soft-spoken man, popular with students and teachers alike. "We are here in an attempt to reach the truth about the missing money."

In a steady, quiet voice he reviewed for Encyclopedia and Sally the background of the case.

Each year, dues from all the school's clubs were put in the bank by the treasurer of one of the clubs. This year the deposits were made by the treasurer of the Service Club—Oliver.

Before Oliver had set out for the bank, Mitch had handed him an envelope with money from the Letterman's Club, of which Mitch was treasurer. Mr. Bertram, the club's advisor, had signed his name across the sealed flap of the envelope.

Oliver had put the envelope into his schoolbag along with those from the other clubs. On his way to the bank, he had stopped at the Chinese restaurant.

Because it was raining, he had decided not to go to the duck pond with a takeout order. Instead, he sat down at a table in the rear room.

A minute later, Mitch and Kate came in and took a table near his. It was after the lunch hour, and the three kids were alone in the room.

Mr. Gerard looked at Oliver, and then at Kate and Mitch. "Now," he said, "we come to the point of disagreement. I want your side first, Oliver."

Oliver cleared his throat nervously.

"After I'd sat down at the table, I noticed my

hands were dirty," he said. "So I asked Mitch and Kate to watch my schoolbag while I washed them. It was the only time I let my schoolbag out of my sight till I reached the bank and found the Letterman's Club envelope missing."

Mr. Gerard thanked Oliver politely. Then the principal invited Kate and Mitch to tell their side.

"Oliver never spoke a word to us in the restaurant," Kate insisted. "When we got there, he was holding an envelope to the light. He slit it open with a table knife and peered inside. At that point he noticed us. He slipped the money from the envelope into his pocket, grabbed his schoolbag, and raced outside."

Mr. Gerard brought his fingers together and pressed the tips against his chin thoughtfully. "Does anyone have anything to add?" he inquired.

Encyclopedia raised his hand. "Sir," he said. "May I ask a question?"

"If you think it will help," Mr. Gerard answered.

"I'd like to ask Kate and Mitch if Oliver had placed his food order?"

"No," Mitch said. "Just as we sat down, a waiter brought a menu to his table. Find the waiter. He must have seen Oliver with the money in his hand."

"You can't find the waiter, and you know it!" Oliver cried. "The restaurant went out of business!"

"We do have one piece of evidence," Mr. Gerard said. He held up an envelope, slit open along the flap. "This is the envelope that held the Lettermen's Club money, according to Mr. Bertram, the club's advisor. He recognized it by his signature on the back."

Kate said, "When Oliver jumped up and ran out of the restaurant, he left the empty envelope behind."

Sally leaned toward Encyclopedia. "It looks very bad for Oliver," she whispered.

"Wrong," replied the detective. "It looks very bad for Kate and Mitch."

WHY?

(Turn to page 55 for the solution to "The Case of the Chinese Restaurant.")

The Case of the Thermos Bottle

On Saturday, Encyclopedia and Sally biked to the elementary school.

The Parent-Teacher Association was holding its summer carnival. Money from the ticket sale would help buy a new air conditioner for the cafeteria.

The detectives each bought a dozen tickets. They had started down a row of booths when they heard Benny Breslin calling to them.

They turned toward the athletic field. A large crowd had gathered to watch the chicken-flying contest. Benny had emerged from the crowd and was fast approaching them. He had a hen under one arm.

"What happened to the worm race?" Sally asked him.

"It's been dropped," said Benny. "Too many kids stepped on opponents' worms last year."

Encyclopedia remembered. Bugs Meany alone had stepped on five worms. Bugs had been boiling mad. He had painted a caterpillar to look like a worm. But the day of the race, it turned into a butterfly. His worm, Fast Ernie, finished next to last.

"How are you doing, Benny?" inquired Sally.

"Queen Cluck here is leading," answered Benny, patting his hen. "If she keeps it up in the the finals, I'll win. First prize is two tickets to the Crest Theater."

"Has Bugs entered a hen?" asked Encyclopedia.

"If he has, it's probably a baby eagle with its claws trimmed," said Sally.

As she spoke, Bugs and several of his Tigers came out of the school. Bugs was carrying a large green thermos bottle, the kind Encyclopedia's mother filled with a hot or cold drink and took on picnics.

"I smell a rat," said Sally.

"Uh-uh," said Benny. "Bugs is trying to make up for being such a poor sport last year. He got Adler's Sporting Goods to donate a baseball glove. He's holding a drawing for it at noon."

"I don't trust him," insisted Sally. "Bugs stands for everything he thinks you'll fall for."

"He can't pull any tricks today," said Benny. "Too many parents are here."

A whistle blew. Mr. Pardee, a fifth-grade teacher, called for the finalists in the chicken-flying contest.

"Boys and girls," he shouted. "Prepare to start your chickens!"

The detectives wished Benny happy landing.

They should have spoken to the hen. Queen Cluck refused to come out of the starting pad, a mailbox.

Benny pleaded. Benny coaxed.

After two minutes, Queen Cluck came out—backward. A hen named Juliet won with a flight of 137 feet, 9 inches.

"Maybe I'll win the baseball glove," said Benny glumly.

The detectives followed him to a table near the library door, where Bugs Meany and his Tigers were selling chances. The baseball glove rested on the table beside a can of root beer.

Benny gave Bugs two tickets and received a slip of paper with a number on it. Bugs wrote the same number on a Ping-Pong ball. He dropped the ball into a box made of clear plastic.

Something bothered Encyclopedia. The green thermos bottle stood under Bugs's chair—yet Bugs sipped from the can of root beer.

"I just made it," said Benny to Encyclopedia. He clutched his slip of paper with the number 114 on it. "I bought the last chance."

It was noon and time for the drawing.

Bugs strutted in front of the plastic box. "I've asked Miss Spottswood to blindfold my buddy, Duke Kelly," he announced.

Miss Spottswood, the school nurse, and Duke Kelly made their way through the crowd. Miss Spottswood wrapped a strip of heavy white cloth around Duke's eyes.

"Watch closely, everybody," sang Bugs. "Are you ready, Duke?"

"Ready," replied the blindfolded Duke. He raised both hands to show they were empty.

Bugs was quick to call attention to Duke's short sleeves. "Nothing is up them," he sang. "Duke Kelly is one boy you can trust!"

"Horsefeathers," snorted Sally. "Duke is so crooked he has to screw on his hat."

Miss Spottswood guided Duke's right hand to the box of Ping-Pong balls. He felt around for a full minute.

"Duke is stirring up the balls," Bugs explained to the crowd. "We don't want you to think the winning ball is stuck on top."

Duke suddenly pulled out a ball. Ripping off his blindfold, he held up the ball so everyone could read the number—81.

"Do you all see it?" Bugs yelled. "Eighty-one! Who's won this beautiful major-league baseball glove?"

"Me!" shouted Rick Larsen. He rushed up to Miss Spottswood and showed her his slip with "81" on it. She gave him the baseball glove and shook his hand.

"It's a set-up," exclaimed Sally. "Rick Larsen is Bugs's pal."

Encyclopedia didn't answer. He was staring

thoughtfully at the large green thermos bottle under Bugs's chair.

Sally stamped the ground. "Encyclopedia! If you can't prove the drawing was fixed, Bugs will end up with the baseball glove himself!"

"No, he won't," said Encyclopedia. "He should never have sipped from the can of root beer. He forgot the thermos bottle was in plain view."

WHAT DID ENCYCLOPEDIA MEAN?

(Turn to page 56 for the solution to "The Case of the Thermos Bottle.")

The Case of the Crowing Rooster

Thursday evening Encyclopedia was trimming the bushes in front of his house when Lisa Periwinkle raced by on her bicycle.

"What's the hurry, Lisa?" called the detective.

"I'm on my way to make my fortune," Lisa hollered. She skidded to a halt and regarded Encyclopedia with interest. "Aren't you going, too?"

"Where?"

"The city dump," answered Lisa. "Wilford Wiggins called a meeting there for seven-thirty. He has a big deal just for us kids."

"The lazy con artist," mumbled Encyclopedia.

Wilford Wiggins was a high school dropout who began his day by going back to sleep. In the afternoon he figured ways of fast-talking the neighborhood children out of their savings.

"Wilford didn't tell me about the meeting," Encyclopedia observed.

"He's mad at you," Lisa replied. "You always squelch his big money-making deals. Frankly, sometimes I don't trust him myself."

“You can never trust Wilford,” Encyclopedia said. “He might be telling the truth.”

Lisa’s face showed uncertainty. “He promised to make us kids so much money we’d be rolling in it,” she said.

“Wilford’s an expert in rolling,” Encyclopedia said. “He has to stuff his mattress with golf balls to roll out of bed.”

“Then come to the dump,” Lisa urged. “You might keep me and the other kids from losing our money.”

“I suppose I’d better go along,” Encyclopedia said. “I’ll get my bike. Won’t be a second.”

It was just seven-thirty when they arrived at the city dump. The first shades of sunset were beginning to close in.

Wilford stood facing the crowd of children. Beside him was a youth of about eighteen who wore an overcoat with a bulge in it.

Wilford flung up one hand and then the other, as if to prove he was on the up-and-up.

“Gather ’round, friends,” he called. “That’s it, step closer. I don’t want you to miss hearing how you can”—he chuckled mysteriously—“feather your nest.”

The children murmured with excitement and inched closer. Bugs Meany and two of his Tigers elbowed their way to the front.

Wilford said, “Allow me to introduce my partner,

Bill Canfield."

The youth beside Wilford bowed. He drew a rooster from under his overcoat and set it on the ground. Then he took a tiny box from his pocket. The box had two knobs.

Wilford cried, "You're thinking, 'What does this tiny box do?' I'll tell you, my friends. It controls roosters. It's Bill's secret ray!"

"I'll make the rooster crow by sending rays to its brain," Bill announced. He turned the knobs on the tiny box.

The rooster stretched its neck and crowed. It crowed twice more within a minute.

Bill turned the knobs back and tucked the rooster into his overcoat.

"I could make this rooster crow hundreds of times in an hour," he proclaimed. "But I don't want to wear out the poor bird in a mere demonstration."

Wilford was fairly dancing with glee. "You saw Bill do it! You saw his box send out secret rays that made the rooster crow three times!"

"You're full of baloney," jeered Bugs. "That's a trained rooster."

"You can't *train* a rooster, friend," Wilford asserted. "The rays made him crow."

"So what?" cried Bugs. "What's Bill going to invent next? An electric spoon?"

"Bugs is right," Lisa whispered to Encyclopedia. "What good is a ray that makes a rooster crow?"

"I'm sure Wilford has something else up his sleeve," answered Encyclopedia.

Wilford's eyes were gleaming. He had played his audience to a fine pitch of doubt. Now he was ready to turn the doubt into belief.

"Bill is developing a ray to control hens," he declared. "Hens are smarter than roosters. So the hen ray takes longer to work out."

"Hens don't crow," shouted Lisa. "They cluck."

"How right you are!" Wilford trumpeted. "Hens cluck . . . and they lay eggs. Bill is perfecting a ray to make hens lay eggs on command!"

The children suddenly grew still.

"I'm on the brink of success," Bill declared. "But I've run out of money to complete the research. So my pal Wilford called this meeting to give all his young friends a chance to buy a share of my hen ray. With your help, I'll finish the project, and you'll reap the rewards."

"An ordinary hen lays about three hundred eggs a year," Wilford said. "Using the ray, a person can make a hen lay two or three or even ten times that number!"

The children understood what that would mean. Farmers all over America—all over the world—would buy the ray. Starvation would be a thing of the past. And everyone would make a bundle of money.

"Don't miss out," Wilford called. "Step right up.

Buy a share in Bill's invention for only five dollars. A year from now you'll thank me with every breath you take."

"I have ten dollars with me," Lisa said to Encyclopedia. "Should I buy two shares?"

"You'd be buying two shares of nothing," replied the detective.

WHY WASN'T ENCYCLOPEDIA FOOLED?

(Turn to page 57 for the solution to "The Case of the Crowing Rooster.")

The Case of the Secret Recipe

Beauford Twitty was eleven, and crazy about potatoes. He was the only person in the United States who ran a potato museum. Admission was by invitation only.

"You're invited to the museum tomorrow at noon," he told Sally and Encyclopedia before the regular Friday afternoon touch football game. "I'm holding a potato-tasting hour to introduce Tubers à la Twitty!"

"What's that?" Sally asked politely.

"Tubers à la Twitty is a secret recipe for preparing the world's newest potato," Beauford answered. "I can't tell you more now."

"How about one tiny clue?" Encyclopedia requested.

"Not about the recipe," Beauford said. "I don't want you to form an opinion before you taste it. But I can tell you about the potatoes that I'll use. They're superspuds."

He explained. His Grandfather Twitty, who had a farm in New York, had been trying for years to breed a better potato. He had finally succeeded.

"Those potatoes are the best," Beauford said. "Grandpa sent me a bagful to test on the all-important kids' market. So I'm trying them out on you and some of my other friends. Tomorrow is D-Day."

"I'm sure Tubers à la Twitty will be delicious," Sally said breathlessly.

"It will be sensational!" Beauford proclaimed. "It will make the name of Twitty famous in the field. Look at Bismarck, Melba, Napoleon, Tetrazzini, Caruso, and Reuben. They gained undying fame. Why? Because recipes were named after them!"

Encyclopedia nodded knowingly. It was the best he could do when Beauford got carried away by his favorite subject, potatoes.

Beauford started for the door and stopped.

"I almost forgot," he said. "I have another surprise. My grandpa sent me a big potato with the autographs of all the Yankee pitchers. I'll display it at the tasting tomorrow."

With that he departed, walking lightly, as if he were stepping on potato chips.

A little before noon on Saturday, the detectives presented themselves at Beauford's front door. Already there were the other guests: Flo Landis, Darlene Cutler, Sean McCoy, and Farnsworth Grant.

At exactly twelve o'clock, Beauford opened the door.

"Come in and look around," he said. "I'll need another few minutes with Tubers à la Twitty."

The potato museum was in the basement. Strewn all about were potato bags, mashers, sacks, peelers, and even an old plow. There were also jars of Colorado beetles—the potato farmer's number-one enemy—and examples of some of the world's thousands of potato varieties.

"I've cleaned up the kitchen," Beauford called down. "We'll eat as soon as I've set the table."

"Let us help you," Sally shouted.

The guests climbed the stairs and went into the kitchen. It was spotless. Everything had been put away.

"My folks let me use the kitchen, provided it was clean when they returned from Glenn City this afternoon," Beauford said.

The guests did not stand around admiring the cleanliness. Each one found something to do. Darlene got the silverware. Sean and Farnsworth found glasses and filled them with water. Flo got out a bottle of ketchup. Sally fetched the paper napkins.

"You can take these," Beauford said to Encyclopedia, handing him a pair of candlesticks. "They'll add the proper touch of class."

When the table was set, Beauford put an old record on the phonograph. The scratchy sounds of Louis Armstrong tooting "Potato Head Blues" filled the dining room.

In the center of the table was a large bowl sealed across the top with aluminum foil. "Behold!" exclaimed Beauford. He whipped off the aluminum foil with a sweep of his arm. In the bowl were french fries.

Beauford grinned. "What did you expect, potato pancakes Rhineland style? Or *pommes de terre farcies*? You shouldn't ruin magnificent potatoes with fancy cooking!"

The french fries were passed around. Farnsworth reached for the ketchup. Beauford howled in pain.

"You've got to taste them pure!" he cried.

The french fries were gobbled pure. They were the best french fries the guests had ever tasted.

"Think what a boon to the fast-food industry my grandfather's potatoes will be," Beauford said, beaming with pleasure.

"What about the potato with the autographs of the New York Yankee pitchers?" asked Farnsworth, who at heart was a Chicago Cubs fan.

"Coming up," Beauford said. He hurried to the basement and brought back a small sack. Carefully he reached inside and pulled out a potato.

It was naked. There wasn't a single autograph on it.

Beauford sank weakly into his chair. "I've been robbed," he gasped.

"Who knew about the potato with the

autographs?" Sally asked.

"Only you six," Beauford replied dully.

"Encyclopedia," Sally whispered. "Say something! Ask a question!"

Encyclopedia wondered if Sally thought he was a detective or a magician. Still, he did have one important clue. . . .

"Was the back door unlocked today?" he inquired.

"Y-yes," Beauford replied. "The doors are never locked during the day if someone is at home."

"Then excuse me," Encyclopedia said. He went outside and walked around the house. He stopped to peer into the kitchen.

When he returned to the dining room, he spoke to one of the guests.

"Would you kindly return the potato you stole?" he said softly.

WHO WAS THE THIEF?

(Turn to page 58 for the solution to "The Case of the Secret Recipe.")

The Case of the Boy Juggler

Excitement had gripped Encyclopedia's neighborhood for weeks. Talent scouts for a new television program, *Young America*, were coming to Idaville to hold tryouts!

One of Encyclopedia's closest pals, Fangs Liverright, had been practicing an act in secret. He refused to talk about it. He would say only that he did "jaw and juggle."

On the great day, Encyclopedia and Sally went to the civic auditorium to watch Fangs perform. As they entered the lobby, a tall woman narrowly missed bumping into Sally.

The woman wore a yellow dress and carried a yellow suitcase. She hurried on without a word.

The detectives looked around for Fangs. They found him bending over a water fountain.

"Thanks for coming," he said. "I can use the support."

"We'll clap like a family of seals," Encyclopedia said.

Sally gazed around at the other contestants. "Aren't you a bit young?" she asked Fangs.

"Everyone else is a teenager."

"I don't expect to win today," Fangs said matter-of-factly. "I'm after experience. I want to go to college free."

"Roll that past us one more time," requested Encyclopedia.

"If I'm satisfied with my juggling today," Fangs said, "I'll work on it during the next seven years so I can get a scholarship."

"Colleges don't give scholarships for *juggling*," Sally protested.

"Boy, are you ever out of it," Fangs said. "These days colleges hand out scholarships for anything."

He lowered his voice. "Wait'll you see my secret act. I juggle three apples and take bites in midair. At the end, I'm juggling three apple cores."

"Wow!" cried Encyclopedia. "That's *core*-dination!"

"The hard part is working with objects of unequal weight," Fangs said. "You have to use different force. But having a pair of front teeth like mine is an advantage."

"Switch to candy apples and you'll win a scholarship to Harvard or Yale," Sally said.

"I want to go to Oberlin," stated Fangs.

A man in a white sport jacket came onto the stage. He announced the start of tryouts.

"The acrobats are first," Fangs said. "Then come the dancers and jugglers. I'd better begin loosening up."

He excused himself and went into the cloakroom. The first pair of acrobats had completed their turn when he emerged. He was pale.

"M-my apples are gone," he stammered in disbelief. "I've searched everywhere. Somebody stole them!"

The detectives pressed him for more information. All he could tell them was that he had carried his apples into the auditorium in a small, dusty yellow suitcase that he'd found that morning in the attic. He had put the suitcase on a shelf in the cloakroom twenty minutes ago.

"A woman with a yellow suitcase left as we came into the auditorium," Sally said.

"Did the suitcase have a zipper?" asked Fangs.

Sally thought a moment. "No, it had clasps."

"Then it wasn't mine," Fangs said.

"Can't you get more apples?" inquired Encyclopedia.

"There isn't time," answered Fangs. His expression hardened. "Besides, I'd rather find the dirty thief. And when I do . . ." His lip curled above his powerful front teeth.

"Button up," cautioned Encyclopedia. "How many other jugglers are in the tryouts?"

"Two," answered Fangs. "Archie Longmire and Claire Foss."

"Archie and Claire are afraid Fangs might outclass them," declared Sally. "They have the most to gain if he can't perform. Let's question them."

Encyclopedia was not nearly so eager as Sally to jump into the case. Archie Longmire was a warm and friendly tenth grader who juggled plates. Claire Foss was only thirteen, but she was sturdy, and as warm and friendly as an iceberg kissing an ocean liner. She juggled bowling balls.

Fangs spotted Archie and Claire standing together in a corner of the auditorium. Sally marched straight up to them.

"Fangs came here with his juggling equipment in a suitcase," she said. "Now the suitcase is missing."

"Gee, that's a shame," Archie said. "Will he be able to go on?"

"You know I won't!" blurted Fangs.

"I'm sorry," Archie said. "But I never saw him with a suitcase."

"Me neither," said Claire. She scowled at Encyclopedia. "Are you *accusing* anyone?"

"No, no, no," replied Encyclopedia as fast as he was able. "We thought you might help us find the thief. Did you notice anyone leaving with a small suitcase?"

"Heck," said Archie. "Kids with suitcases and shopping bags have been coming and going all morning."

"Then we'll have to comb every inch of the building," Encyclopedia said heavily. "The suitcase is old and dusty, and the thief is certain to have left fingerprints."

"Wait a second," said Claire. "Now that I think about it, I did see someone suspicious. A woman in a bright yellow dress was leaving in one big hurry as you came in. She had a suitcase!"

"I saw her, too," said Archie. "She was in an awful rush. She nearly bumped into Sally. And she had a yellow suitcase like Fangs's."

"That wasn't my suitcase," Fangs said. "Mine has a zipper."

Sally turned to Encyclopedia. "It'll take us a week to search all the rooms in the building," she said. "We're not even sure if the thief hid the suitcase or made off with it."

"Why don't you ask the thief?" suggested Encyclopedia.

WHO WAS THE THIEF?

(Turn to page 59 for the solution to "The Case of the Boy Juggler.")

The Case of the Marathon Runner

Cicero Sturgess, Idaville's greatest child actor, staggered into the Brown Detective Agency and fell on his face.

Encyclopedia and Sally rushed to his side. As they stooped to aid him, Cicero jumped up and grinned.

"I fooled you!" he cried.

"You're not hurt?" Sally said. "What's the big idea?"

"The marathon race tomorrow," Cicero answered. "It will launch my stage career nationwide. Think of the publicity! 'Ten-Year-Old Actor Proves His Grit!'"

Sally gasped in astonishment. "You've entered the Idaville marathon?"

"Every step," Cicero replied. "When I collapse at the finish line, I'll be the center of attention."

He went into his finish-line act again, lurching like a man dying of the bends.

"There'll be waves of interviews," he said, straightening. "You know, radio, television, newspapers. I'll feed 'em a few choice lines about the conquest of pain and how I never quit. Then I'll bring up my acting career."

"Why should anyone interview you?" inquired Sally. "How can you hope to win?"

"Who said anything about winning?" asked Cicero.

"Well, what—"

"I've been training for three days," declared Cicero. "Plenty of overeating and no exercise. I'm in shape, and I'm ready. I plan to finish last."

Encyclopedia wished him luck.

"I'll need it," replied Cicero. "Anyone can win a marathon. It isn't so easy to finish last."

With that, he departed the way he had entered, staggering toward an imaginary finish line.

The next day, Sunday, the detectives biked to City Hall, where the marathon was to begin. Cicero, the youngest runner, worc number 84.

At two o'clock, the starter fired his gun. Encyclopedia and Sally watched till the runners were out of sight. Then they peddled to the seven-mile mark of the race.

Nearly two hours later, Cicero jogged by. He was locked in a struggle for last place with a woman wearing a neck brace and a man running backward.

"Keep it up, Cicero!" Sally shouted. To Encyclopedia she said with a sigh, "This may go on all night."

There was nothing to do but telephone their parents and say they would be home late. They went to a movie and ate dinner at Andy's Pizza Parlor.

Night had fallen when they stopped outside the Idaville Concert Hall, a mile from the finish, and cheered a few runners laboring past. Encyclopedia pointed to the large electric sign above the concert hall: "Tonight Only—Railroad Brotherhood Band Concert."

"We might as well go in," he said. "Cicero won't be coming by for another hour."

The detectives bought tickets and forgot about the time as they sat listening to the music. Just before the intermission, the band struck up a medley of state songs.

"This piece sounds like 'I've Been Workin' on the Railroad,'" Sally said. "But the program lists the title as 'Eyes of Texas.'"

"Both songs have the same tune," Encyclopedia explained, glancing down at Sally's program. He noticed her watch. It was nearly nine o'clock!

"We may miss Cicero!" he gasped. "C'mon!"

By taking a shortcut, they reached the finish line of the marathon in three minutes. The area was nearly deserted.

All the spectators had gone home, and the last officials were preparing to leave. The first-aid station had closed. A single reporter chatted idly with men from a television truck as they packed up their gear.

Suddenly someone shouted, “Hold everything! Here comes one more!”

A TV man grabbed a camera and aimed it down the shadowed street at a small figure—number 84. It was Cicero! The young actor wobbled like a broken top and fell across the finish line.

“He’s done it!” yelled Sally. “He’s lost to everyone!”

“He took more than seven hours,” marveled Encyclopedia.

Surrounded by a storm of congratulations, Cicero quickly livened to his task. He struck pose after pose, gestured, bowed, and likened the hardships of a marathon to getting ahead in acting.

He was delivering lines from his most recent dramatic appearance when Millicent Potter, number 76, crossed the finish line. All at once, Cicero was without an audience. Everyone dashed to welcome the new loser.

Millicent, a pretty tenth grader, seemed astonished by her sudden importance. She hadn’t realized, she said, that she was the only runner still on the course.

“This is my first marathon, and I didn’t think I could make it,” she said, panting. “Then I passed the concert hall while the Railroad Band was playing ‘Eyes of Texas.’ The music inspired me.”

She wiped her face with a forearm and smiled bravely at the TV camera.

"I started humming as I ran the last mile," she said. "Music gives me strength. Music is my life. I hope to be a singer after I graduate high school. But it's so hard for an unknown to get a break today. . . ."

Cicero was listening to her in shock. She had not only stolen his great moment, she was using it to advance *her* career.

"I feel sorry for Cicero," Sally said. "What tough luck to have outrun Millicent."

"He didn't," replied Encyclopedia. "When the officials learn what Millicent did, they'll declare Cicero the rightful last-place finisher."

WHAT DID ENCYCLOPEDIA MEAN?

(Turn to page 60 for the solution to "The Case of the Marathon Runner.")

The Case of the Diving Partner

Otis Dibbs biked up to the Brown Detective Agency. He wore sneakers and a bathing suit, and he was dry all over.

Otis was usually soaking wet. During the summer he dove for golf balls that had been hit into the water hazards on Idaville's two golf courses. He sold the balls to golfers who liked to use old balls near the water.

The work had its dangers. Golfers sometimes mistook him for an alligator. They waited to bop him on the head with a club when he came up for air.

"Golly, Otis," said Encyclopedia. "What are you doing here? You're way off course."

"I want to hire you," said Otis. He placed twenty-five cents on the gasoline can beside the boy detective. "Helga the Horrible—I mean, Helga Smith—is taking over my business."

"That lazy windbag?" exclaimed Sally. "Every night she must dream she found a job. She looks tired even in the morning."

“The only time Helga lifts a finger is when Miss Casey tells her to,” said Encyclopedia.

Miss Casey was the manicurist at the Ace Beauty Parlor. She did Helga’s nails every week.

“Helga muscled in on my business,” said Otis. “I do all the work, but she takes half the money.”

“We’ll look into it,” said Sally. “Where is she?”

“I left her at the sixth hole of the country club half an hour ago,” said Otis.

The three children got their bikes. Otis talked about the case as they pedaled to the country club.

Diving for golf balls was hard work, but worth the effort. Golfers always needed cheap balls to use on water holes.

Also, Otis found a lot of clubs, which angry golfers threw into the water. Putters were the most common. But once in a while he found a complete, matched set.

The business of selling the old balls and clubs had been good until last week. Then Helga came by and gave him some advice.

“She slapped me on the back and told me how much better I’d do with her as a partner.”

“The slap on the back was to help you swallow what she said,” grumbled Sally.

“You know it,” agreed Otis. “You’ve got to get rid of that big do-nothing.”

“We’ll find a way,” promised Encyclopedia. “Don’t worry.”

But Encyclopedia worried. Helga was seventeen and could have gone to a reform school on a scholarship. She had a grin like a saber-toothed tiger.

At the country club, Otis showed them where to park their bikes. Then they walked quickly to the sixth hole.

Helga was just climbing out of the pond to the right of the fairway. She wore an orange bathing suit and goggles. She waved to Otis and pointed to a sign near the water.

CAUTION: DIVERS AT WORK

"How do you like it?" she called. "It was delivered a few minutes ago. What a work of art! Cost us only twenty dollars, little partner."

Otis gagged. "T-twenty d-dollars?"

Encyclopedia stared at the sign. It looked as if it had been painted on the back of a motorcycle.

"Otis doesn't need a sign," snapped Sally. "And he doesn't need a partner."

"Wrong, my dear," replied Helga. "With both of us diving, we can double our business."

"You haven't dived *once*!" protested Otis. "All you do is lie in the shade and count the balls I bring up. But when I sell them, you grab half the money."

"Temper, temper," Helga warned. She tapped the thick, smooth tips of her fingers together. Then she made a show of examining her manicured nails.

Encyclopedia looked from Helga to the only shaded place near the pond—a clump of six oak trees.

"Helga could have been resting there, waiting for Otis to return," thought the boy detective. "She could have seen use before we saw her. All she would have had to do was slip into the water and pretend she'd been busy diving."

"A business," Helga said, "has to be run with brains. Now, take the sign. Golfers won't mistake us for alligators anymore. That's thinking the Helga Smith way."

"Fore!" a man shouted from the fifth tee. "Fore!"

"Duck!" cried Otis. A ball whizzed past Encyclopedia and splashed into the pond.

"Go get it, partner," commanded Helga.

"Why don't you?" said Sally.

"I'm tired out," Helga answered. "I've been diving for a solid hour." She nodded at a green pail beside Otis's clothes. "Found nine balls and a putter while you were gone."

"I found the putter and those balls this morning!" screamed Otis.

"Are you calling me a liar?" Helga rose slowly to her feet, breathing heavily on her right fist.

Otis retreated five steps, just breathing heavily.

"Nobody calls me a liar," said Helga. "You prove I didn't find those balls, and I'll bow out. You can have the business all to yourself."

"And if he can't prove you lied?" demanded Sally.

Encyclopedia wished Sally hadn't asked the question.

"If he can't," repeated Helga, grinning her sabertoothed-tiger grin. "If he can't, I'll find myself another partner. And I'll flatten this one's nose till it looks like an all-day pizza."

Otis uttered a low moan.

"Encyclopedia," said Sally, "help Otis!"

"You mean prove that Helga didn't dive for those balls?" inquired the boy detective. "That's easy."

WHAT WAS THE PROOF?

(Turn to page 61 for the solution to "The Case of the Diving Partner.")

The Case of the Overstuffed Piñata

Encyclopedia was walking along Main Street one day early in September when he sighted trouble.

Tim Gomez was standing halfway down the block and looking madder than a flea on a stone dog. He was holding a box and a piece of wrapping paper in one hand, and he was glaring across the street at Bugs Meany.

Bugs was leaning against the wall of the post office and balancing a toy bull in his hand. He was laughing and joking with three of his Tigers—and watching Tim.

"Encyclopedia!" Tim cried. "Am I glad you came along."

"What's going on?" the detective inquired.

"That no-good Bugs stole my bull!" exclaimed Tim.

He explained. His Aunt Maria, who lived on a farm in the western part of the state, had sent him a papier-mâché piñata shaped like a bull. Because there was postage due, he'd had to go to the post office to pick up the package. As he opened it on the sidewalk, Bugs had come by and grabbed the bull.

"Now Bugs says it's his," Tim grumped. "All I have left is the box and the wrapping paper."

Encyclopedia tried to catch up. A piñata, he knew, was a decorated figure or jug. In Latin American countries piñatas filled with gifts are hung from the ceiling and broken on holidays. Children, wearing blindfolds, hit them with sticks until they break and the presents fall out.

The detective squinted across the street at the piñata bull Bugs was holding. Except for the horns, which were black, the bull was covered all over with little curls of tissue paper in strips of yellow, orange, and pink.

"I was in Hector's Department Store half an hour ago," the detective said. "I noticed a counter of piñatas—papier-mâché bulls and clay jars—because a lady accidentally knocked a jar and two bulls onto the hard floor. The jar broke, but the bulls just bounced."

"Did the bulls look like mine?" Tim asked anxiously.

"One of them did," replied Encyclopedia. "There were more like yours on the counter."

"Rats," Tim grunted. "Now Bugs can lie his head off. He'll swear that he bought my piñata bull at Hector's."

"And the salespeople will never remember whether he bought one or not," Encyclopedia added.

"Well, mine is different," Tim said. "My aunt always makes a little hole in the piñata and stuffs a lot of candy inside. She stuffs it so full it doesn't rattle."

"That's it!" Encyclopedia remarked. "Bugs won't know about the hole, and so you—"

"No good," Tim broke in. "My aunt seals the hole up so well that you can't see where it is from the outside. I'd have to break open the piñata to prove it."

"Bugs will never let you do that," commented Encyclopedia.

The detective closed his eyes and did some heavy thinking. He thought of how to trap Bugs into admitting he had stolen the bull from Tim.

Suddenly his eyes opened. "Let's have a talk with Bugs," he said, smiling.

As Encyclopedia and Tim started across the street, Bugs took a better grip on the bull.

"Get lost," he growled at the detective, "or I'll pound you so hard on the top of the head you'll have to reach up to pull on your sneakers."

Encyclopedia was quite used to Bugs's welcomes. Calmly he said, "Tim claims you stole that bull from him."

"Man, oh, man!" Bugs wailed. "I'm accused of everything! Listen, I haven't stolen a thing for weeks. I've gone straight."

"You couldn't go straight if you walked a

tightrope!" yelped Tim.

Bugs made a fist, but then caught himself. "For your information, I just bought this bull at Hector's Department Store," he said.

"Come on, Bugs, wasn't it quite a while ago that you were at the store?" Encyclopedia said. "And haven't you done some other shopping since then?"

"I don't know what you're getting at," Bugs snapped. "I bought this bull just a few minutes ago. I was heading home when I saw this crazy kid coming out of the post office with nothing but that empty box and the piece of wrapping paper."

"I ought to wrap his head, the big liar!" Tim whispered to Encyclopedia.

"Sssh," Encyclopedia whispered back, watching Bugs's fist.

"I guess someone sent him a package with nothing in it," Bugs went on. "When he saw my bull, he pretended it belonged to him. Fat chance. Someone sent him an empty package to match his empty head."

"Are you sure you didn't do anything else after you bought the bull?" Encyclopedia asked.

"I told you once, didn't I?" Bugs's voice had risen shrilly. "What's the matter? Don't you believe the word of an honest boy?"

"Yes, I do," Encyclopedia said. "That's why I believe Tim."

WHAT MADE ENCYCLOPEDIA SO SURE?

(Turn to page 62 for the solution to "The Case of the Overstuffed Piñata.")

Solution
THE CASE OF THE MISSING GARLIC BREAD

The Tigers knew that if you eat parsley, it will take away bad breath, even the smell of garlic.

But they forgot they had eaten with their hands.

Unfortunately for them, Encyclopedia was on the case. He told Sally to sniff the hands of each Tiger.

"Garlic," she said over and over as she went from Bugs to Duke to Spike to Rocky. "Yuk!"

"You Tigers nearly got away with it," said Encyclopedia. "If you had washed your hands with strong soap, the garlic smell would have disappeared.

Sally laughed. "The Tigers wash their hands? Never!"

Trapped by their own mistake, the Tigers all chipped in enough money to pay Josh back for the ingredients for chocolate cake and garlic bread.

Solution
THE CASE OF THE BUBBLE GUM SHOOTOUT

Teresa wasn't the "perfect stranger" Malcolm made her out to be. She had come *prepared* to blow bubble gum.

Encyclopedia realized immediately that the peanut butter wasn't her lunch, as she'd pretended. There was nothing to spread it on or eat it with.

What was the peanut butter for? Encyclopedia knew.

Peanut butter is the handiest thing to use for *untangling hair stuck with bubble gum*.

After being faced with the evidence, Malcolm admitted he had cheated. Teresa was his cousin—the under-sixteen girls' bubble gum champion of nearby Glenn City.

Cephas lost the shootout, but he won the bike.

Solution
THE CASE
OF THE CHINESE RESTAURANT

Kate wanted revenge on Oliver because he had beaten her in the election for treasurer of the Service Club.

So she got Mitch to help her steal the money belonging to the Lettermen's Club while Oliver was in the rest room. Then they blamed Oliver.

Encyclopedia saw through their story immediately. Oliver could not have opened the envelope "with a table knife."

In Chinese restaurants, knives are not part of the table setting. They are brought to the table only after the customer has ordered a steak or something that requires a knife to cut.

And Oliver had not yet ordered. As Mitch himself stated, the waiter was just bringing Oliver a menu when he and Kate sat down!

Solution
THE CASE OF THE THERMOS BOTTLE

Bugs did not use the large thermos bottle. So why had he brought it to the carnival?

Encyclopedia quickly got Miss Spottswood to examine the winning Ping-Pong ball. As he had suspected, the ball was cold.

Bugs had marked the ball at home and put it into the freezer for two hours. He brought it to the carnival in the thermos bottle to keep it cold.

Shortly before noon, he slipped the cold ball into the box with the other balls. Duke Kelly felt around till he found it.

Rick Larsen gave back the glove. Another drawing was held—without Bugs. Benny Breslin won.

Solution
THE CASE OF THE CROWING ROOSTER

Encyclopedia noticed what the other children had overlooked—what really made the rooster crow. It wasn't the ray.

Bill had kept the rooster hidden under his overcoat, in darkness. When he took it out, the bird saw the first shades of *sunset*. But it thought, after being kept in the darkness, that the time of day was *sunrise*.

Hence the rooster did what roosters do naturally at sunrise. It crowed.

Thanks to Encyclopedia, none of the children gave Wilford money for the phony ray.

Solution
THE CASE
OF THE SECRET RECIPE

Flo was the thief.

She had gone to Beauford's house twenty minutes early and looked into the kitchen window. When she saw that he was busy making french fries, she had sneaked into the museum by the back door.

After stealing the potato with the autographs and substituting an ordinary one, she had returned to the house shortly before noon for the tasting.

She confessed when Encyclopedia pointed out her mistake—the bottle of ketchup.

She would not have brought ketchup to the table unless she knew that Beauford's Tubers à la Twitty was not some fancy dish but simply french fries.

Solution
THE CASE OF THE BOY JUGGLER

The thief was Archie, who wanted to win the juggling contest.

When Encyclopedia remarked that the thief's fingerprints would be on Fang's suitcase, Archie became frightened. He tried to cast suspicion on the woman in the yellow dress. He said, ". . . she had a yellow suitcase like Fangs's."

But earlier Archie had said he hadn't seen Fangs's suitcase. So he couldn't have known it was yellow unless he was the thief!

Foiled by his own words, he showed Fangs where he'd hidden the suitcase.

Fangs had just enough time to take the stage. But without a warm-up, he gagged on an apple and had to withdraw.

Solution
THE CASE OF THE MARATHON RUNNER

Millicent lied when she said she had "passed the concert hall while the Railroad Band was playing 'Eyes of Texas.'"

She knew the sign out front gave the name of the band. So, running past, she would have assumed the song was "I've Been Workin' on the Railroad."

Only if she had been *inside* the hall and seen the program could she have known the song was "Eyes of Texas." Both songs, as Encyclopedia told Sally, have the same tune!

Thanks to Encyclopedia, the truth came out. She had left the race after two miles and had not come back until the last mile.

Millicent was disqualified. Cicero was declared the official loser.

Solution
THE CASE OF THE DIVING PARTNER

Helga thought that if Otis, Encyclopedia, and Sally saw her getting out of the pond, they would be fooled. They would believe her lie that she had been in the water for "a solid hour."

However, she overlooked Encyclopedia's sharp eye for clues.

Remember that when she tapped her fingers together, Helga unmindfully called attention to her smooth skin? That was her downfall.

After an hour in the water, the skin would have been wrinkled!

Trapped by her own fingertips, Helga retired from the diving business.

She said the work was too hard.

Solution
THE CASE OF THE OVERSTUFFED PIÑATA

In Hector's Department Store, Encyclopedia had seen three piñatas fall off the counter. The clay jar broke. But the two papier-mâché bulls bounced. Had they been filled with candy, they would have been too heavy to bounce.

When Bugs claimed he had bought the piñata bull at Hector's, Encyclopedia got him to say he had just bought it "a few minutes ago." Therefore, it should still have been *empty*!

But Tim's aunt had stuffed it with a lot of candy. The number of stamps on the wrapping paper showed that the package had weighed more than a papier-mâché bull would weigh by itself.

Encyclopedia challenged Bugs to go to the store and weigh the piñata bull. Knowing it was full and heavy, Bugs refused.

But he gave Tim back the bull.